WORKBOOK

CLIENT GETTING P.L.A.N.

How to Get All the Clients You Can Handle
Without Cold Calling or Spending a Dime on Marketing

DREW LAUGHLIN

IMPORTANT

This workbook is part of the complete "Client Getting P.L.A.N." online training course.

If you are not a member of this training program then this workbook will probably not make sense to you.

Discover the power of CGP here:

ClientGettingPlan.com

Disclaimer

We don't believe in get rich programs – only in hard work, adding value and serving others. Our training programs, courses, books, videos, etc. are intended to help you improve your business skills and encourage you to take action so you can build and grow your business. Our products and programs take work, effort and discipline just like any worthwhile endeavor or professional continuing education program. Please don't invest in our products and programs if you're a "get rich quick" kind-of-person; we only want serious people who want to work hard to build their business. As stipulated by law, in promoting this and all our programs we use illustrative numbers only and we cannot and do not make any results guarantees or give professional or legal advice. In short, you are guaranteed to get results or earn an income. We provide information and its up to you what you do with it. However, we do guarantee your satisfaction and you have a full 30 days from purchase to evaluate any of our products and request a refund, unless otherwise noted on the specific product or program sales page.

If we reference a third party product, service, website etc. you need to know two things. First, our reference is one of just that – reference. If we feel something is useful and can benefit you we will tell you about it. Secondly, in some cases – not all - when we refer or mention a third party product, program, website, etc. we may be compensated for referring you IF you decide to purchase that item.

Testimonials

"Drew Laughlin knows how to get clients and more importantly, he knows how to teach YOU to get clients. His training is professional, interesting and nothing is left to chance. Plain and simple, if you follow his method you will get new clients. If you want to grow your business, I would strongly recommend the Client Getting Plan."

- Andrew Mason Owner, Advertising Accomplished, LLC

"I would recommend the Client Getting Plan by Drew Laughlin to both new and experienced Consultants who want to ramp up their ability to generate quality clients in a consistent manner instead of hit or miss cold prospecting techniques. It worked very well for me and my business!"

- Judy Casey The Best Business Consulting

This training program opened my eyes to a new way of getting clients. For an introvert like me, it was hard to do, but I keep saying to myself even if I only know 25% of this, it's 25% more than the people I am talking to. Great course, great people. Thanks Drew"

"The greatest thing I have got out of the course to date is that I now, very nearly have a complete presentation that I know I'll be happy, proud & confident to deliver to roomfuls of prospects. Thanks Drew"

"I have gotten great value of information and great ideas on what direction one would need to when accessing new clients Highly endorse if you want to take yourself to the next level."

- Pat Brosnan

"Drew, the Client Getting Plan is fabulous! Everything from the presentation of the course to the content in the course is TOP NOTCH. I did my first lunch and learn and the results were awesome. You provided everything someone could possibly need to be successful with this. I added 9 people to my lists (some signed up for every list I have) and one person wants a strategy session. Thanks for putting this together for us!"

- Glennette Goodbread

"Before working with Drew and the Client Getting Plan, I was struggling with finding clients. When Drew introduced me to CGP I took immediate action and got my first L&L scheduled very quickly. For that first L&L there were 15 businesses and I closed 3 mobile website design clients! In less than 4 months I now no longer need to go looking for clients! However, if I did I would turn on the Client Getting Plan. and I would be 100% confident I would get as many clients as I needed. I highly recommend working with Drew. His laid back no fluff teaching style keeps you focused on the tasks that need to be done. Just take action, believe in yourself and who knows, one great contact can fill your funnel for a very long time!"

- Dino Iannuzzi PinItMarketing.com

Want Free Stuff?

Sign up for all kinds of free goodies at:

DrewLaughlin.com

Table of Contents

Step 1

Construct Your Lists

Three Lists

1. R_____ N_____ T_____
2. F_____ T_____
3. P_____ B_____ C_____

You can also use it for:

- C_____ U_____
- C_____ of _____
- Various Associations
- Any group or organization that has members that can benefit from your message!

Topics

Right Now Topics

- Your _____
- Talk about in your _____
- Helps _____ the most
- A _____ you actually like talking about
- What makes you _____!

Future Topics

- You _____ to learn about
- Are _____
- Are _____

Bank Contacts

Decision Makers

- _____

Search

- _____
- _____

Success Factors

Success Factors #1

- Contact _____
- Get _____ and _____

Success Factors #2

- _____ your list creation
- Use_____
- And_____

Outsourcing

Guidelines

- Be _____ but don't ____ _____
- Ask for _____
- Don't hire someone with no _____
- Pay through _____ only _____ the project is complete

Mistakes to Avoid

- Thinking a _____ or _____ is invaluable or insignificant
- _____ your _____
- Trying to get it _____
- Not using _____ _____
- Ignoring _____ and _____
- Stopping before you have _____ contacts

Step 1: Action Steps

1. Create your ____ ___ _____ list

2. Create your _____ _____ list

3. Create or _____ an _____ to create your ____ _____ _____

Step 2

Contact Your List

Creating a Unique Sales Message

Creating a message for the bank contact

- Ensure it provides value to _____ _____

- Show them how it's _____ and _____

- Focus on _____, not _____

Write your own USM:

_____

_____

_____

Getting Past the Gate Keeper

Write your own script:

_____

_____

_____

_____

_____

_____

Speaking to the Main Contact

Write your own script:

_____

_____

_____

_____

_____

_____

Leaving a Voice Mail

Write your own voice mail message:

_____

_____

_____

_____

_____

Questions to Ask

List out questions you'll ask:

_____

_____

_____

_____

_____

How L&Ls Work

- At their own _____, which preferably has a _____.
- Ask them to provide _____,or offer to _____ _____ with them.
- The _____ of the event is their responsibility.
- You will provide _____ on the specific topic, any _____, _____ _____ and printed _____.
- Finish with, "I will _____ you again on _____."

Answering Questions You Don't Know the Answer To

- It's okay to say, "_' _ ___ _____."
- Ask what they _____.
- Tell them "That is typically _____ by _____," and ask if that _____ for them.
- Create a _____ _____ so you can research and be more prepared next time.

Scheduling a Follow Up Call

- Schedule a time to _____ the contact _____.

- Goal: to have them commit to the _____ _____.

- This will be a _____- __- _____ meeting.

- Also to schedule the first _____- ____- _____.

Rookie Mistakes

- Not following _____ _____.
- Wanting to "_____ _____ _____."
- Being reluctant to _____.
- Unnecessary worries about not being able to _____ _____.
- Trying to be _____.

What Not to Do

- Make _____.
- _____ it.
- Using a _____ service too soon.

Step 2: Action Steps

1. Create _____.
2. Customize and practice _____ _____.
3. Plan your _____ _____ and _____ to it!

Step 3

Create Your Presentation

Lunch and Learn Basics

- Create an irresistible _____.

- Make it _____ and powerful.

- Time length should be about _____ to _____ minutes long.

- Describe one _____ and one _____.

- Don't put your _____ on every _____.

Presentation Outline

- In your intro tell them why _____ are the best one to teach them.

- What they will _____ and the _____ that holds for them.

Main content should include:

    1.) S _____

    2.) M _____ P _____

    3.) C _____

- Rookie _____

- _____ steps.

Presentation Enhancers

- Relatable _____ and _____.
- S _____
- Your own _____.
- One-page _____.

2 Ways to Handle Non-Believers

1. A _____, A _____, and A _____

2. A _____, A _____, and A _____.

Rookie Mistakes and What Not to Do

- Your presentation should be _____ and not _____.
- Making a L&L that's too _____.
- Going into excruciating _____.
- Not enough time for _____ & _____.
- Not providing a valuable _____.

Step 3: Action Steps

1. Create a _____ title

2. Use the _____ _____ to create your first L&L presentation

3. Create a _____-_____ FIB worksheet

Step 4

Customize, Practice, and Prepare

Best Practices for Presentations

- _____ Yourself.
- Practice at least _____ to _____ times.
- Tweak to ensure presentation fits into _____ to _____ minute time intervals.
- Extract _____ from recording and listen to it repeatedly so you can know it ____ _____.
- Practice in front of _____ and _____.

What to Look for in Practice Recordings

- Identify _____s and _____s.
- Recognize _____ parts.
- Points that should be _____ or _____.
- Areas to _____.
- Look for awkward _____ and _____.
- Make sure you have _____ and that it's coming through.
- Check _____.
- Reduce _____.

What Not to Do

- Making a presentation _____ and not _____ it.
- Not _____.
- Assuming the _____ has everything covered.

Step 4: Action Steps

1. _____ your presentation for your first L&L

2. Get your first practice session _____

3. Get familiar with the "_____ _____" and add/remove things as needed

Step 5

Confirm and Commit

Confirmation Script for the Phone

- Keep conversation _____ and _____ _____.
- Using a _____, cover all the necessary _____.
- These include: _____, _____, _____, and other details.

Write your own call script:

_____

_____

_____

_____

Confirmation Script for Email

- Only email if you don't _____ _____.

- Using a _____, to cover all the details in the email.

- Follow up with a phone call _____ day before _____.

Write your own email:

_____

_____

_____

_____

Rookie Mistakes and What Not to Do

- Neglecting to _____.
- Not making sure _____ is covered.
- Not _____ yourself.
- Only sending confirmation by _____.
- Ignoring the _____.
- Making _____ to keep you from committing to the L&L.

Step 5: Action Steps

1. _____ your L&L
2. _____ to your L&L

Step 6

Convey Your Message and Close Deals

10 Tips to Convey Your Message

1. Keep your intro _____.

2. Tell _____.

3. Keep it _____.

4. C _____.

5. Keep it _____.

6. Have a one _____.

7. Never _____ your slides.

8. Skip _____ and _____.

9. Place the focus on the _____.

10. Have _____ at the end.

Getting Clients

- Be _____.
- Do not use _____.

It's all about getting to the next action. That might be:

  - Getting _____.
  - Additional _____.
  - _____ "I'll think about it" prospects.

Rookie Mistakes and What Not to Do

- Converting back to _____ _____ tactics.

- Making it about _____ and not _____ problems.

- _____ _____ sales tactics.

- Not _____ on presentation or selling skills.

- Being someone other than _____.

- Stressing over the _____.

- Putting a lot of _____ on others.

Step 6: Action Steps

1. Continue to _____ your presentation until your live L&L

2. Practice your _____ close

3. _____ what you want and go make it happen!

Step 7

Convert to Webinar

Webinars and Benefits

- A webinar is a _____ conducted over the _____.

Benefits

  ▪ Saves _____ because you can do it from your _____ or _____.

  ▪ Saves _____ without _____ or _____.

  ▪ _____ for attendees.

Webinar Weaknesses

- Not as _____ as L&Ls.
- _____ for "Next Actions" are not as high.
- _____ not as strong.
- _____ are responsible for getting attendees.
- Could be more _____ to get attendees.

How and When to Use Webinars

- _____ to L&Ls
- _____ to L&Ls
- Introduce new _____ or _____ after _____
- After you conduct _____

Automated vs. Live Webinars

Automated:

- Benefits are that they are run _____.

- _____ webinars can be recorded and used as _____.

- Most attendees _____ _____ if webinars are live or automated.

Live

- _____ way to do webinars.

- More _____.

- Some attendees _____ live webinars.

- Better _____.

Webinar Presentations

- Same as _____, but can be _____.
- Webinars can be _____, _____, or _____ minutes.
- But still, _____ is usually more.

Rookie Mistakes and What Not to Do

- Starting webinar before doing _____.

- Putting too _____ in webinar.

- Using only _____ or _____ _____.

Step 7: Action Steps

1. After you've done a _____ of live L&Ls' test the water to see if _____ are a good fit

2. Do a live _____ and _____ it

3. Use the _____ to create your _____ _____

Next Step

One of the most effective ways to grow your business - I mean really grow your business - is not to have a coach but a mentor who has been there and done that. A person who can not only guide you along your journey but hold you accountable when things need to get done.

If you're tired of struggling to take your business to the next level then check out our private, limited membership into our V.I.P. Mentorship program.

ClientGettingPlan.com/vipmember

Did you find this training beneficial?

Want more like it?

The best way to learn about my other products and training programs is to go to:

DrewLaughlin.com

www.ingramcontent.com/pod-product-compliance
Lightning Source LLC
Chambersburg PA
CBHW081738170526
45167CB00009B/3866